You Put What In My Dessert?!

From Alaska, The Best Sauerkraut and Cabbage Recipes In The World

by Alicia Loveland

Publication Consultants
Since 1978

PO Box 221974 Anchorage, Alaska 99522-1974
books@publicationconsultants.com
www.publicationconsultants.com

ISBN 978-1-59433-244-9
Library of Congress Catalog Card Number: 2011931666

Manufactured in the United States of America.

Dedication

You Put What in My Dessert is dedicated to Michael, my son, for giving a thumbs up, or down, on my recipes and to Ron, my husband, because he sacrificed his waistline for my dessert section, washed continuous mountains of dishes as I experimented with desserts, made many trips to the store for forgotten ingredients, and helped me sort through all of my recipes this last year.

Acknowledgement

I acknowledge and gratefully thank Diane Drashner, the illustrator, for this book. I love her whimsical illustrations/ they added to the fun of writing this cookbook.

Recipes

Vegetables and Side Dishes...................................31

Why I Wrote The Book

People have asked, "Why a sauerkraut cookbook?"

There is no short answer.

I was born in Palmer, Alaska (the Matanuska Valley) where summer sun shines endlessly, and cabbages grow to 100 pounds. In an annual contest, the winner of the largest cabbage wins $2000.00. It could be said that I have a history with cabbage.

When I was eight, my family moved to Cantwell, Alaska. The temperatures there were colder, the soil poorer, and the chance of growing anything other than flowers was pretty slim. We learned how to survive on the homestead. A homesteader improvised with what they had, or could find since stores were not "just down the road." That's where cabbage came in. It stored well, and if fresh wasn't on hand, a person could make sauerkraut or buy canned. Things were purchased in case lots, so cans of vegetables were the norm for villagers of Alaska.

Cabbage has been heralded as a cancer inhibitor in the *Journal of Agricultural and Food Chemistry,* is loaded with vitamin C, only has 11 calories per service, and goes in anything. It can be fried, boiled, baked, frozen, canned, or dried and then ground in a food mill and used to thicken soup. Making it into sauerkraut is an added bonus because it is ready to use, as you will see in my dessert section.

I can't be all wrong about the greatness of cabbage since sauerkraut got its start over 2000 years ago when the laborers building the Great

Wall of China pickled cabbage in wine to supplement their diet. Genghis Khan came along and liked it so much he took it back to fortify his Tartars as they plundered their way through Europe. The Germans liked the pickled cabbage and named it sauerkraut, meaning sour cabbage. Captain Cook knew of its importance when he carried sauerkraut on his ships to ward off scurvy.

Sauerkraut is a mainstay in our household. I keep rinsed, drained, chopped (in a food chopper or snipped with scissors) sauerkraut in the refrigerator. It is as important to me as sourdough starter is to an Alaskan homesteader.

After judging a World Federation of Competitive Eaters cabbage eating contest in Palmer a few years ago, I decided this cookbook needed to be written. I felt so sorry for those contestants eating plates of plain, boiled cabbage by the pound. I wish I could have spiced it up for them with a little caraway seed, dill, mint, mustard seed, savory, or tarragon.

Soups and Salads

Soups and Salads

VEGETABLE-BARLEY SOUP

1 c. cabbage, shredded
½ c. celery, sliced
½ c. cut green beans
1 T. margarine
2 ¼ c. water
3 pkts. instant beef broth and seasoning mix
1 sm. bay leaf
dash each of thyme, salt, pepper

½ c. onion, chopped
½ c. zucchini, sliced
½ c. canned whole tomatoes
½ c. mushrooms, sliced
½ c. instant barley

½ c. carrot, sliced

In 2-quart saucepan, heat margarine until hot. Add chopped vegetables and mushrooms; cook over medium heat, stirring occasionally, until cabbage begins to wilt, about 10 minutes. Add remaining ingredients and bring to a boil. Reduce heat, cover, and let simmer for 30 minutes, stirring occasionally. Serves 4.

POLISH SAUSAGE SOUP

1 lb. Polish sausage, cut into ½-inch pieces
5 med. potatoes, cubed   2 med. onions, chopped
2 lg. carrots, cut into ¼-inch slices
1 (46-oz.) can chicken broth
1 (32-oz) can sauerkraut, rinsed and drained
1 (6-oz.) can tomato paste

Combine all ingredients in a slow cooker; stir. Cover. Cook on high 2 hours and then low 6-8 hours. Serve with rye bread. Serves 8.

SAUERKRAUT SOUP

4 T. olive oil	4 T. butter
3 L onions, chopped	2 T. paprika
2 lbs. sauerkraut, drained	1½-qts. water
1 stalk celery, sliced	1 carrot, chopped
1 tsp. caraway seeds	3 tsp. sugar
½ c. red wine	1 tsp. dill weed
1½ tsp. salt	½ tsp. pepper
3 cloves garlic, minced	
2 (14-oz.) cans tomatoes with juice	
1 (4-oz.) can mushroom slices	

Heat the olive oil and butter in a large pot. Sauté the onion and garlic until they are golden. Add the rest of the ingredients and let simmer for at least one hour. If the soup is too thick, add more water. Serves 6.

CABBAGE SOUP

1 T. oil	1 T. butter
1 clove garlic, chopped	1 L onion, chopped
4 c. shredded cabbage	6 c. chicken stock
2 T. soy sauce	1 c. rice
2 tsp. salt	¾ c. cheddar cheese, grated

Heat the oil and butter in a large pot. Sauté onion and garlic until they are limp. Add cabbage and cook for 5 minutes. Stir to keep from burning. Add stock and soy sauce. Bring to a boil. Add rice and salt. Lower heat and simmer for 30 minutes. Serve with grated cheese. Serves 4.

CABBAGE, HAM, AND BEAN SOUP

½ c. onion, chopped	2 qts. water
2 c. ham, diced	3 c. shredded cabbage
2 (16-oz.) cans tomatoes, chopped and undrained	
1 T. chili powder	
2 (16-oz.) cans pinto beans, undrained	

Sauté onion in a large pot with a little oil. Add the water, ham, cabbage, tomatoes with juice, and chili powder. Bring mixture to a boil and add beans. Lower heat and cook for 30 minutes. Serves 8.

WALNUT ACRES MINESTRONE SOUP

2 qts. beef broth
½ lb. frozen peas
1 pkg. frozen spinach
1 yellow onion, chopped fine
4 cloves garlic, minced
½ T. parsley, dried
1 tsp. salt

2 (15-oz.) cans kidney beans
4 c. cabbage, shredded
4 carrots, chopped
4 stalks celery, chopped fine
½ c. rice
½ tsp. sage
½ tsp. pepper

Put all of the ingredients in a pot and let them cook until the carrots are soft but not mushy.

BASQUE VEGETABLE SOUP

¾ lb. Polish sausage, sliced
8 c. water
1 lg. turnip
1 lg. potato, cubed
1½ tsp. salt
½ T. parsley, dried
1 c. cabbage, shredded
1 (15-oz.) can navy or great northern beans

3 chicken breasts, small
2 carrots, sliced
1 lg. onion, chopped
1 clove garlic, minced
½ tsp. pepper
1 tsp. thyme, dried

In skillet, cook sausage until done. Remove sausage to plate. Cook chicken breasts until done and then cut into cube size chunks. Add the meats, as well as all the other ingredients, to a pot. Simmer until the vegetables are soft, but not mushy. Serves 10-12.

SPICY CABBAGE-BEEF SOUP

1 lb. ground beef
5 c. cabbage, chopped
2 (16-oz.) cans red kidney beans
1 green bell pepper, chopped
4 beef bouillon cubes
½ tsp. salt

1 lg. onion, chopped
2 qts. water
3 (8-oz.) cans tomato sauce
¾ c. picante sauce
1½ tsp. cumin, ground
¼ tsp. pepper

Brown ground beef and onion over medium heat in a skillet. Drain. Put the meat, onion and all other ingredients into a slow cooker. Cook on low 6 to 8 hours or on high 3 to 4 hours. Serves 10.

SAUERKRAUT AND POTATO SOUP

1 lb. smoked Polish sausage, cut into ½-inch pieces

5 potatoes, cubed   2 onions, chopped

2 carrots, ¼-inch slices   6 c. chicken broth

2 (15-oz.) cans sauerkraut, rinsed and drained

1 (6-oz.) can tomato paste

Put all ingredients in a slow cooker. Cook on low 8 hours
Serves 8.

CZECHOSLOVAKIAN CABBAGE SOUP

1 c. onion, chopped	3 carrots, chopped
2 cloves garlic, minced	1 bay leaf
2 lbs. beef short ribs	1 tsp. thyme, dried
½ tsp. paprika	8 c. water
4 c. cabbage shredded	2 (14-oz.) cans tomatoes
1 tsp. salt	½ tsp. Tabasco sauce
1 T. parsley, dried	3 T. lemon juice
3 T. sugar	1 (16-oz.) can sauerkraut
4 beef bouillon cubes	

Brown short ribs under broiler. Put all ingredients in a slow cooker
on low for 8 hours, or high for 4 hours. Serves 12.

BEET AND SAUERKRAUT ASPIC

2 env. gelatin, unflavored	½ c. cold water
2 c. hot water	1 tsp. salt
1½ T. sugar	
2 c. canned beets, chopped	
1 med. apple peeled and chopped	
1 (15-oz.) can sauerkraut	1 T. bottled horseradish

Soften gelatin in cold water. Stir into hot water until dissolved. Add
salt and sugar. Cool. Combine with other ingredients and mix. Turn
into a mold and chill until firm. Serves 6.

SWEET AND SOUR CABBAGE-APPLE SALAD

1 med. head cabbage, sliced thin
1 lg. apple, peeled and cubed   1/8 tsp. ground cloves
1 sm. sweet green pepper, sliced into thin strips
1 sm. yellow onion, chopped fine
½ c. red wine vinegar   1 T. honey
½ tsp. caraway seeds   1/8 tsp. black pepper

Combine cabbage, apple, green pepper and onion in a large heat proof bowl. In a small saucepan over medium heat, cook the vinegar, honey, caraway seeds, black pepper and cloves until it boils for 1 minute. Pour the hot mixture over the salad and toss. Refrigerate for 30 minutes before serving. Serves 4.

SURPRISE CABBAGE SALAD

2 pkgs. lemon Jell-O	2 pkgs. lime Jell-O
4 c. hot water	2 c. miniature marshmallows
2 c. crushed pineapple	2 c. pineapple juice
2 c. mayonnaise	3 c. cabbage, shredded
2 c. whipped cream	2 c. walnuts, chopped

Dissolve the packages of Jell-O in the 4 cups of hot water. Add the marshmallows. Stir until dissolved. Add the crushed pineapple and juice. Add enough water to pineapple juice to make 2 cups. Add salad dressing and shredded cabbage. Refrigerate until it starts to set. Add the whipped cream and nuts. Refrigerate until ready to serve.

PINEAPPLE COLESLAW

½ c. sour cream	½ c. mayonnaise
2 tsp. sugar	1 T. onion, grated
1 tsp. lemon juice	2 c. cabbage, shredded
1 c. carrots, shredded	½ c. cashews
¾ c. pineapple tidbits, drained	

In a small bowl, combine the first 5 ingredients. In a large bowl, combine the next 4 ingredients. Pour the small bowl dressing ingredients over the salad in the large bowl and mix well. Refrigerate to blend flavors. Serves 6.

COLESLAW WITH CHEESE

¼ c. sour cream
¼ c. mayonnaise
1 tsp. Dijon mustard
1½ T. white vinegar
¼ tsp. ground cumin
¼ tsp. salt
1/8 tsp. pepper
2½ c. cabbage, shredded
1 med. carrot, shredded
½ green bell pepper, cut into thin strips
½ c. green onion, sliced
½ c. dill pickles, diced
4 oz. Jack cheese, diced
1/8 tsp. cloves
1/8 tsp. allspice
¼ tsp. caraway seeds

Combine the first 7 ingredients and pour that mixture over the rest of the ingredients. Mix all together and refrigerate. Serves 4.

DILLY CORNED BEEF SALAD

3 c. cabbage, shredded
2 c. deli corned beef, cubed
2 c. potatoes, cooked and cubed
½ c. dill pickle, chopped
¼ c. onion, sliced thin
½ c. mayonnaise
1 tsp. prepared mustard

Combine all ingredients in a large bowl. Mix well. Refrigerate to blend flavors. Serves 6.

CABBAGE SALADA

1 (15-oz.) can red kidney beans, drained
1 (15-oz.) can garbanzo beans
½ small head cabbage, cubed
¼ c. onion, chopped
2 T. green pepper, chopped
1 clove garlic, minced
1½ tsp. salt
½ tsp. dry mustard
½ tsp. sugar
1 tsp. pepper
5 slices bacon, cooked until crisp
¼ c. oil
¼ c. vinegar

Place first 5 ingredients in a large bowl. Mix well. Combine garlic, salt, mustard, sugar, pepper, oil, and vinegar. Pour over bean mixture and toss lightly. Refrigerate. Before serving, garnish with diced pieces of bacon. Serves 6.

CELERY SEED SLAW

3 tbs. cabbage, coarsely shredded
½ c. carrot, shredded
½ c. green pepper, chopped
1 c. sugar   1 c. vinegar
1 T. salt   1 tsp. celery seed

Combine cabbage, carrot, and green pepper in a large bowl. In a saucepan, combine the sugar, vinegar, salt and celery seed. Bring to a boil. Pour over cabbage mixture and toss. Cover and refrigerate overnight. Can be kept for one month in the refrigerator if put in quart jars with lids. Serves 12.

STEIRISCHER KRAUT SALAT

1 med. head cabbage, thinly sliced
3 tsp. caraway seeds   ¼ tsp. salt
1 c. bottled Roquefort dressing
1/8 tsp. pepper   ½ c. cranberries, diced

Combine cabbage, caraway seeds, dressing, cranberries, salt and pepper in a bowl. Cover and refrigerate for one hour before serving. Serves 6.

GINGER SWEET COLESLAW

½ med. head red cabbage, shredded
1 green pepper, thinly sliced
½ med. red onion, thinly sliced   ½ tsp. salt
⅓ c. apple cider vinegar   3 T. olive oil
1 T. soy sauce   ½ tsp. fresh ginger, minced
1 tsp. sugar   sesame seeds

Combine cabbage, green pepper, and red onion in large bowl. Mix vinegar, oil, soy sauce, ginger, salt, and sugar. Pour over salad mix and toss well. Cover and refrigerate to blend flavors. Garnish with sesame seeds before serving. Serves 4-6

GREEK CABBAGE SALAD

1 med. head cabbage, shredded
2 cloves garlic, minced   ½ lb. feta cheese, crumbled
⅓ cup olive oil   3 tsp. dill weed
1/8 tsp. salt   1/8 tsp. pepper

Combine garlic, olive oil, dill weed, salt and pepper. Pour it over cabbage and feta cheese. Toss lightly. Refrigerate to blend flavors.

DANISH COLESLAW

4 c. cabbage, shredded   1 tart apple, peeled and diced
1/8 c. onion, chopped   2 T. fresh chives, chopped
¾ c. sour cream   ½ c. blue cheese, crumbled
⅓ c. mayonnaise   2 tsp. white vinegar
2 tsp. lemon juice   ½ tsp. dill weed
1 pinch paprika   ¼ tsp. salt
1/8 tsp. pepper

Mix all ingredients in a large bowl. Cover and refrigerate to blend flavors. Serves 4-6.

CRUNCHY CABBAGE SALAD

4 c. cabbage, shredded   1 c. carrots, shredded
½ c. red bell pepper, chopped   ½ c. water chestnuts
¼ c. green onions, sliced thin   ½ c. cashews
1 (2-oz.) can sliced mushrooms, drained
1 (3-oz.) can chow mein noodles ⅓ c. mayonnaise
⅓ c. sour cream   1 T. soy sauce
1 tsp. sugar   ½ tsp. ginger
1/8 tsp. garlic powder   1 dash Tabasco sauce

Combine cabbage, carrots, bell pepper, water chestnuts, onion, and mushrooms in a large bowl. Mix mayonnaise, sour cream, soy sauce, sugar, ginger, garlic powder and Tabasco sauce in a small bowl. Pour dressing over salad mixture and toss. Refrigerate to blend flavors. Add noodles and cashews just before serving. Serves 6.

OLD FASHIONED CABBAGE SLAW

½ tsp. dry mustard   ½ tsp. celery seed
2 T. sugar   1 tsp. salt
¼ tsp. pepper   1 T. onion, finely chopped
4 tsp. oil   ⅓ c. white vinegar
4 c. cabbage, shredded

Mix the mustard, celery seed, sugar, salt, pepper, onion, oil, and vinegar. Pour over cabbage and mix well. Serves 4-6.

PINEAPPLE COLESLAW

2 oz. milk   2 T. white vinegar
½ tsp. salt   1 T. mayonnaise
1 tsp. Dijon mustard   2 tsp. sugar
2 c. cabbage, shredded
½ c. crushed pineapple in juice

Combine all ingredients and mix well.

CLASSIC COLESLAW

1 c. mayonnaise   3 T. lemon juice
2 T. sugar   1 tsp. salt
6 c. cabbage, shredded   1 c. carrots, shredded
¼ c. green pepper, finely chopped

Combine ingredients and mix well.

SCANDINAVIAN FRUIT-FILLED SLAW

2 oranges, sectioned   2 apples, chopped
2 c. cabbage, shredded   1 c. seedless green grapes
½ c. whipping cream, whipped 1 T. sugar
1 T. lemon juice   ¼ tsp. salt
½ c. mayonnaise

Combine oranges, apples, cabbage, and grapes in a bowl. Fold whipped cream, sugar, lemon juice, and salt into mayonnaise. Stir whipped cream mixture into fruit mixture. Refrigerate. Serves 6.

SWEET SLAW

1 (8-oz. can sliced peaches, drained
1 c. cabbage, shredded   1 sm. carrot, shredded
½ c. miniature marshmallows
3 to 4 T. mayonnaise   1 tsp. lemon juice

Reserve 4 peach slices. Cut remaining peaches into ½-inch pieces; mix with cabbage, carrot, marshmallows, mayonnaise, and lemon juice. Refrigerate 1 hour. Serve over lettuce leaves, and garnish with reserved peach slices. Serves 4.

CITRUS SLAW

1 c. mayonnaise
⅓ c. frozen orange juice concentrate, thawed
2 tsp. sugar   ¼ tsp. salt
¼ tsp. pepper   6 c. cabbage, shredded
2 c. carrots, shredded   ½ c. raisins

Combine mayonnaise, orange juice concentrate, sugar, salt, and pepper. Stir in remaining ingredients. Cover and chill. Makes about 4 cups.

SAUERKRAUT-APPLE SALAD

1 c. sauerkraut, rinsed and drained
1 sm. apple, chopped   ½ cucumber, chopped
1 tsp. onion, finely chopped   1 T. oil
¼ c. walnuts, chopped   1 pinch dill seed
1 pinch fennel   1 pinch salt

Mix rinsed and drained sauerkraut, apple, cucumber, and onion together. Add oil, walnuts, dill seed, fennel and salt. Mix all and refrigerate.

HAWAIIAN SLAW

⅔ c. Wish Bone Russian Dressing
1sm. head cabbage, shredded
1 (8-oz.) can pineapple chunks, drained
1 orange, diced   ¼ c. green pepper, chopped

Combine all ingredients in a large bowl; chill. Serves 8.

APPLE-CARROT SLAW

4 c. cabbage, shredded	2 c. carrots, shredded
2 c. Red Delicious apple, unpeeled and chopped	
⅔ c. mayonnaise	2 T. sugar
⅓ c. white vinegar	1 tsp. celery seeds

Combine cabbage, carrots, and apple. Mix mayonnaise, sugar, vinegar and celery seeds together. Combine dressing with the vegetable-fruit mixture. Serve on leaves of cabbage. Serves 8.

WALDORF SLAW

5 c. cabbage, shredded	2 c. apples, diced
⅓ c. raisins	½ c. mayonnaise
¼ c. Wish-Bone Sweet 'n Spicy French Dressing	

Combine cabbage, apples and raisins in a large bowl; toss with mayonnaise and dressing. Serves 12.

PINEAPPLE COLESLAW

12 c. cabbage, shredded	1 c. miniature marshmallows
2 (20-oz.) cans pineapple chunks, drained	
¼ c. drained pineapple juice	¼ c. sugar
1½ c. Miracle Whip	¾ c. walnuts, chopped
2 bananas, sliced	

Mix pineapple juice, sugar, and Miracle Whip in blender. Combine cabbage, marshmallows, pineapple chunks and walnuts in a large bowl. Pour dressing over fruit mixture and mix. Just before serving, slice bananas and add to mixture. Serves 25 (½ c. portions).

CABBAGE SLAW WITH NECTARINES

1 c. plain yogurt	1 T. brown sugar
1 T. lemon juice	4 c. cabbage, shredded
1 c. nectarine or peaches, sliced	½ c. peanuts, chopped

Combine yogurt, brown sugar, and lemon juice in a large bowl. Add cabbage, nectarine and peanuts. Toss and serve, or refrigerate. Serves 8 (½ c. servings).

CABBAGE SALAD

1 lg. cabbage, thinly sliced	2 lg. onions, thinly sliced
1 med. sweet pepper, thinly sliced	
1 c. sugar	2 T. sugar
1 tsp. celery seed	1 tsp. dry mustard
1 T. salt	1 c. vinegar
¾ c. oil	

Combine cabbage, onions, sweet pepper and 1 c. sugar in a large bowl. Combine 2 T. sugar, celery seed, dry mustard, salt, vinegar, and oil in a small saucepan and bring to a rolling boil. Pour the saucepan ingredients over the vegetables; cover and let stand overnight. Pack in quart jars and refrigerate. Keeps for 1 month.

CHINESE CHICKEN SALAD

½ head cabbage, shredded
2 cooked chicken breasts, cubed

2 T. slivered almonds	2 T. sesame seeds
2 green onions, diced	2 T. sugar

1 pkg. chicken flavored Top Ramen noodles, broken and uncooked

½ tsp. pepper	1 tsp. salt
½ c. oil	3 T. vinegar

Toast slivered almonds and sesame seeds; add to cabbage, onions, and cooked chicken. Mix sugar, pepper, salt, oil, vinegar, and seasoning from Top Ramen noodles; pour over cabbage mixture. Add Top Ramen noodles just before serving.

CORN-CABBAGE SALAD

4 c. cabbage, shredded	½ c. onion, chopped
1 c. cooked corn	½ c. diced sharp cheese
2 T. sliced black olives	1 T. parsley, dried
⅓ c. mayonnaise	2 tsp. prepared mustard
¼ tsp. celery salt	

Combine cabbage, onion, corn, cheese, and olives in a large bowl. Mix parsley, mayonnaise, mustard and celery seed; add to cabbage mix and toss. Serves 6.

KENNICOTT COLESLAW

3 c. green cabbage, shredded   2 c. red cabbage, shredded
1½ c. apples, chopped
1 c. Miracle Whip Salad Dressing
1 T. honey   ½ tsp. cinnamon

Mix all ingredients together and garnish with apple slices. Serves 6.

Vegetables and Side Dishes

VEGETABLES & SIDE DISHES

CABBAGE AU GRATIN

7 lbs. cabbage, coarsely chopped and cooked

2½ cubes butter	1¼ c. flour
2½ tsp. salt	1¼ tsp. pepper
10 c. milk	1 lb. cheddar cheese, grated
6 oz. bread crumbs	3 oz. butter, melted

Melt 2½ cubes of butter in saucepan. Stir in flour, salt and pepper, making a smooth paste. Gradually add milk, blending well. Stir sauce on medium heat until thickened. Alternate layers of cooked cabbage, sauce, and grated cheese. Combine bread crumbs and 3 oz. of melted butter. Sprinkle on top of the cabbage, sauce, cheese mixture. Bake at 350° for about 25 minutes. Serves 50.

HOT CABBAGE

3 c. cabbage, finely chopped	½ tsp. salt
2 T. oil	2 T. Italian salad dressing

Sprinkle cabbage with salt and set aside for 30 minutes. Heat oil in skillet until very hot. Add the cabbage and stir fry about 2 minutes. Remove and add Italian dressing. Serves 4.

SAVORY RED CABBAGE

4 c. red cabbage, shredded	¼ c. vinegar
¾ c. water	¼ c. brown sugar
¼ tsp. ground cloves	2 tart apples, diced
1 tsp. salt	

Combine all ingredients and cook at low temperature until cabbage and apples are tender, about 20 minutes. Serves 6.

GERMAN RED CABBAGE

3 T. bacon drippings   6 c. cabbage, shredded
2 med. apples, peeled and chopped
⅓ c. onion, finely chopped   ¼ c. brown sugar
⅓ c. red wine vinegar   ¼ c. water
1½ tsp. salt   1 tsp. caraway seed
¼ tsp. pepper

Combine all ingredients in 2½ quart glass casserole. Cover with glass lid. Microwave 8 minutes on high; stir well, continue cooking for 8 minutes on high, or until cabbage is crisp-tender. Serves 6.

SPICED RED CABBAGE

12 lbs. red cabbage, shredded (about 3 heads)
2 qts. red wine vinegar   1 c. brown sugar
½ c. mustard seed   ¼ c. whole cloves
¼ c. mace   ¼ c. whole allspice
¼ c. peppercorns   ¼ c. celery seed
1 stick cinnamon

Place cabbage in a large bowl, salting each layer. Cover and let stand in cool place for 24 hours. Rinse and drain well. Combine vinegar, sugar, and mustard seed in a large saucepan. Tie cloves, allspice, peppercorns, celery seed and cinnamon sticks in a cheesecloth bag; add to saucepan with vinegar mixture and boil for 5 minutes. Pack cabbage into hot jars leaving ¼-inch head space. Remove spice bag from vinegar mixture and pour hot liquid over cabbage, leaving ¼-inch head space. Adjust caps. Process quarts 20 minutes in boiling water bath. Yields 5 quarts.

CURRIED CABBAGE

1 tsp. red onion, minced   6 c. cabbage, shredded
2 T. margarine
½ tsp. curry powder (or more for spicier flavor)

Sauté onion until tender. Add curry powder and cabbage; cover, and cook for 10 minutes or until tender. Serves 4.

PIEROGI

¼ lb. margarine	4 c. flour
2 eggs, well beaten	¾ c. milk
¼ c. water	3 T. sugar
3 T. raisins	¼ tsp. cinnamon
4 c. sauerkraut	½ cube margarine
2 med. onions, finely chopped	

In a large bowl, work margarine into flour as for pie crust. Add eggs, then milk and water to make a stiff dough. Knead this on a lightly floured surface. Roll out very thin and cut with a glass or round cookie cutter. Boil sauerkraut for 5 minutes and rinse in cold water. Squeeze juice from sauerkraut. Melt margarine in saucepan; add onions and cook until tender. Add sauerkraut to onions and heat through. Fill dough circles with sauerkraut filling (about 2 tsp. each); fold over one side, and press edges together. Boil in lightly salted water for about 5 minutes. Remove and cool in cold water. Pierogi may be served with sour cream. Yields about 30.

CABBAGE AND NOODLES

4 c. cabbage, shredded	1 T. salt
½ c. oil	½ tsp. sugar
3 c. cooked noodles	¼ tsp. pepper

Mix the cabbage and salt together; let stand 30 minutes. Squeeze out liquid. Heat oil in skillet; add sugar and cabbage. Cook over medium heat until cabbage is tender. Add noodles and pepper; blend thoroughly. Serves 6-8.

APPLE SAUERKRAUT

1 lb. sauerkraut	½ c. unsweetened applesauce
½ c. water	1 sm. onion, chopped
2 tsp. caraway seeds	

Combine ingredients in a saucepan and simmer, covered, for 30 to 40 minutes. Serves 4.

COOKED CABBAGE WITH APPLES

2 T. oil   1 med. onion, sliced
½ med. head red cabbage, shredded
2 cooking apples, peeled and sliced
2 T. raisins   2 T. honey
2 T. red wine vinegar   ½ tsp. cinnamon
½ tsp. allspice   ½ tsp. ground cloves
6 T. plain yogurt

Heat oil in frying pan; brown onion. Add cabbage and applies; sauté 3 minutes. Add raisins, honey, vinegar, and spices; cook over medium heat about 10 minutes, stirring occasionally. Let cool a few minutes and then stir in yogurt. Serves 4.

FRENCH FRIED CABBAGE

½ head cabbage   ½ c. milk
½ c. flour   ¼ tsp. salt
¼ tsp. pepper

Separate inside leaves of cabbage and crisp them in cold water. Drain and dry leaves. Dip leaves in milk, then dip them in flour, salt, pepper mixture. Fry them in hot fat until golden brown. Drain on paper towels and eat while warm.

SWEET AND SOUR SAVORY CABBAGE

1 sm. head green cabbage, sliced
1 sm. head red cabbage, sliced
1 med. Vidalia onion, thinly sliced
½ c. apple cider vinegar   1 T. sugar
1 T. butter   1 tsp. coriander
½ tsp. cardamom

Cut cabbage into thin slices. Combine the sugar and vinegar and set aside. Heat the butter in a pot over medium heat; add onion and sauté 3 minutes. Add cabbage and toss well with the onion. Add the sugar mixture to the pot along with the spices and mix well. Cook, stirring frequently, for 5 minutes, or until cabbage is soft. Serves 4.

THAI STIR-FRIED

2 T. lime juice	⅔ tsp. red pepper flakes
a little oil	6 c. cabbage, shredded
¼ c. onions, chopped	2 cloves garlic, crushed
⅓ c. coconut	¼ c. peanuts

Heat a little oil in a wok over high heat. Add the lime juice, red pepper flakes, cabbage, onions and garlic; stir fry until cabbage is hot through. Stir in the coconut and peanuts. Serves 4.

CURRIED CABBAGE AND PEAS

1 med. head cabbage, shredded	3 T. oil
1 tsp. crushed dried red chilies	½ tsp. ground ginger
½ tsp. ground cumin	2 bay leaves
1 tsp. ground coriander	½ tsp. turmeric
2 tsp. salt	1 c. water
2-½ c. frozen peas	1 T. butter
1 T. lemon juice	½ tsp. sugar
½ tsp. mustard seeds	

Heat oil in large skillet and stir in all spices. Heat for 2 minutes, stirring often. Add shredded cabbage and peas and sauté all. Add water, cover, and cook for another 10 minutes. Stir in the butter, lemon juice, and sugar. Simmer, uncovered, until there is very little liquid left. Stir in a little yogurt if desired, and serve with rice. Serves 6-8.

CABBAGE AND ONION WITH GARLIC

2 T. oil	1 lb. red cabbage, shredded
1 lg. onion, cut in half and sliced in thin strips	
2 cloves garlic, minced	1 T. soy sauce
1 T. sesame seeds	

Heat oil in wok. Sauté onion and garlic. Add rest of ingredients and stir fry 5 minutes over medium-high heat until cabbage is crisp-tender. Serves 4.

SPICED CABBAGE

4 T. butter	1 sm. head cabbage, cut into wedges
¼ c. chili sauce	2 T. water
½ tsp. caraway seeds	½ tsp. allspice
½ tsp. salt	¼ tsp. pepper

Put butter in a 10-inch round baking dish and microwave, uncovered, 1 minute on High, or until melted. Roll cabbage wedges in melted butter to coat. Arrange cabbage so the wider portions of the wedges face the outside of the dish. Combine all the remaining ingredients in a small bowl. Spoon over the cabbage wedges. Cover. Microwave on High 10 to 13 minutes, or until cabbage is nearly tender. Let stand 5 minutes before serving. Serves 6.

CABBAGE CASSEROLE

4 c. cabbage, shredded	1 c. celery, sliced
1 can cream of celery soup	⅓ c. milk
4 tsp. soy sauce	1 T. onion, minced
1 dash Tabasco sauce	2 T. butter, melted
½ c. Ritz crackers, crushed	

Cook cabbage and celery in salted water just until tender. Drain. Mix all and put into a casserole dish. Sprinkle with melted butter and crushed crackers. Bake 350° for 40 minutes.

CABBAGE POLONAISE

12 lbs. cabbage, cored and cut into wedges	
3 cubes butter	1½ c. flour
3 tsp. salt	1½ tsp. pepper
12 c. milk	

Parboil cabbage wedges in salted water until partially cooked. Arrange cabbage wedges in baking pans. Add butter to a large saucepan and cook until melted. Stir in flour, salt, and pepper, making a smooth paste. Gradually add milk, blending well. Cook on medium until sauce is thickened. Pour sauce over cabbage wedges, sprinkle with buttered bread crumbs and bake at 350° for about 25 minutes. Serves 50.

GRATIN OF CABBAGE

10 T. butter	4 T. flour
2½ c. milk	1 egg
3 cloves garlic, crushed	salt and pepper to taste
1 med. head cabbage	1 c. Gruyere cheese grated

Melt 4 tablespoons of butter in saucepan and whisk in flour. Let cook over low heat for 3 minute, stirring constantly. Whisk in milk and bring to a boil. Add salt, pepper and crushed garlic. Remove from heat. Beat egg in a bowl and add a small amount of the garlic sauce into the egg. Next, beat the egg mixture back into the garlic sauce. Set aside. Heat 6 tablespoons butter in a deep pan. Toss cabbage in hot butter until it is crisp-tender (not mushy). Fold together the cabbage and garlic béchamel sauce. Pour the mixture into a 2-quart shallow baking dish. Sprinkle with Gruyere cheese. Bake, 350°, uncovered, for 30 minutes until browned and bubbly. Serves 4-6.

CREAMY CABBAGE

6 c. cabbage, shredded	¼ c. onion, chopped
⅓ c. water	½ tsp. salt
3 oz. cream cheese, cubed	½ tsp. celery seed
2 T. butter	paprika, to taste

Cook cabbage, onion, water, and salt for about 7 minutes, or crisp-tender. Drain. Add cream cheese, celery seed, butter and paprika while hot. Serves 6.

GREEN BEANS AND CABBAGE

3 T. butter (not margarine)	1 tsp. coriander
2 c. cabbage (cut into 1-inch cubes)	
1 c. fresh green beans (1 inch long)	

Melt butter in large skillet over medium-high heat until butter turns golden brown; remove from heat. Add cabbage and green beans; toss to coat. Reduce heat to low; cover and cook until vegetables are crisp-tender, stirring occasionally. Before serving, sprinkle with coriander. Serves 4

CABBAGE EN CROUTE

2 T. butter	1 T. sugar
1½ tsp. lemon juice	3 c. cabbage, shredded
½ c. tart apple, shredded	¼ c. onion, chopped
¼ tsp. salt	¼ c. sour cream
5 frozen phyllo pastry sheets, thawed	
¼ c. butter melted	¼ c. dry bread crumbs

In large skillet, melt 2 tablespoons butter. Add sugar and lemon juice; stir until sugar dissolves. Add cabbage, apple, onion, and salt. Cook over medium heat until vegetables are tender, stirring occasionally. Drain. Add sour cream; mix well. Heat oven to 350°. Lightly grease cookie sheet. Place 1 phyllo sheet on prepared cookie sheet. Brush with melted butter; sprinkle with about 2 teaspoons bread crumbs. Continue layering the remaining 4 sheets of phyllo sheets, brushing each with butter and sprinkling the crumbs. Place cabbage mixture in 2-inch wide strips 4 inches from short side of phyllo sheets and 1-½ inches from long sides of sheets. Fold 1-½ inch sides over cabbage. Fold 4 inch side over cabbage mixture. Roll up jelly-roll fashion. Place cabbage roll seam side down. Brush with remaining melted butter. Bake at 350° for 30-35 minutes, or until golden brown and crisp. Allow to stand 5 minutes before slicing. Serves 6.

SAUERKRAUT

20 lbs. mature cabbage heads
½ lb. pickling salt

Wash, quarter, core and shred cabbage. Weigh out 20 pounds of cabbage. Thoroughly mix ½ pound of pickling salt with the cabbage. Firmly pack into a keg or crock pot. The salt draws fluid out of the cabbage. If, after you pack it into the crock, it is not covered in fluid, more fluid can be made by dissolving 2 tablespoons of pickling salt in 1 quart of water. Double bag 2 freezer bags and fill the inner one with water. You will use this as a weight to hold the cabbage down in the fluid, as well as to keep air away from the cabbage as it ferments. Cover your crock with a clean, thin, white cloth. Cover this with a plate to keep everything out. Room temperatures of 68° to 72°F, is best for fermenting cabbage. Fermentation takes anywhere from 3 weeks to 6 weeks, depending on the temperature at which it was cured. Soft kraut may be caused from 500 high of temperatures of yeast on the surface and is caused by being improperly covered. Rotted kraut is usually found on the surface because air got to it during fermentation. Dark kraut is caused by insufficient juice over the kraut, high temperatures during fermentation, long storage period, or exposure to air. It is alright to check your kraut periodically without it rotting. When it is sauerkraut, put it in a big pot and bring to a simmer (185° to 210°F).Do not boil. Pack sauerkraut into hot, clean jars and cover with hot juice to ½ inch of top of jar. Adjust jar lids. Process in boiling water bath (15 minutes for pints and 20 minutes for quarts). Set jars upright, several inches apart, to cool.

.

Main Dishes

MAIN DISHES

CABBAGE STEW

1 lb. ground beef	2 T. oil
2 onions, roughly chopped	½ c. celery, sliced
2 c. cabbage, shredded	1 c. water
1 (15-oz.) can red kidney beans	1 (15-oz.) can tomatoes
1 tsp. chili powder	½ tsp. salt
½ tsp. pepper	3 c. hot mashed potatoes

Brown ground beef in a little oil. Add onions, cabbage, and celery. Sauté. Add water, beans, tomatoes, and seasonings. Cook for 30 minutes, adding more water if needed to keep from burning. Top with mashed potatoes before serving. Serves 6.

SAUERKRAUT DOGS AND MUSTARD SAUCE

2 T. butter	dash pepper
1 tsp. salt	1 T. prepared mustard
1 T. flour	1 egg yolk, beaten
¾ c. milk	1½ tsp. lemon juice
1 (29-oz.) can sauerkraut, undrained	
1 tsp. caraway seeds	1 pkg. franks, heated

In saucepan, melt butter; stir in pepper, salt and mustard. Add milk, gradually. When it comes to a boil, remove from heat and stir some of the milk mixture into a well beaten egg yolk. Add that mixture back to the saucepan and put back on heat at a low setting. When it has thickened, remove and add lemon juice. In another saucepan, heat the undrained sauerkraut with the caraway seeds. Top the sauerkraut with the heated franks and pour the mustard sauce over all.

GRECHEN'S CASSEROLE

1 (20-oz.) can sauerkraut, drained
1 (20-oz.) can sliced apples, undrained
½ c. brown sugar   ¼ c. onion, minced
2 T. butter   2 (12-oz.) cans Spam
2 tsp. prepared mustard

In 2-quart casserole, combine sauerkraut and undrained apples with ¼ cup brown sugar, and onion; dot with butter. Slice Span into 8 to 12 slices; arrange on top of sauerkraut mixture. Combine ¼ cup brown sugar with mustard; spread on meat. Bake, uncovered, 30 to 40 minutes at 400°, or until meat is glazed and sauerkraut is heated through. If canned apples aren't available, use canned pie filling with a little water added. Serves 4-6.

PORK ROAST

3 lbs. pork roast   2 T. brown sugar
3-½ c. sauerkraut, rinsed and drained
1 c. apples, unpeeled and chopped
1 c. carrots, shredded   1½ c. tomato juice

Brown roast in a skillet. Place in a slow cooker. Combine remaining ingredients and pour over roast. Cook on low 10 hours.

SOUTHERN STEW

1¼ lbs. boneless sirloin steak   2 tsp. oil
1 c. onions, sliced   2 cloves garlic, minced
1½ c. canned crushed tomatoes   1 tsp. salt
½ tsp. chili powder   1/8 tsp. ground red pepper
1 c. cabbage, thinly sliced   8 oz. garbanzo beans
¼ c. green bell pepper   2 T. fresh parsley, chopped

Brown steak on each side. Cut into 2-inch pieces and set aside. Sauté onions, garlic, green pepper and parsley in oil. Add all ingredients to a slow cooker; cook on low for 8 hours to 10 hours. Serves 4.

RUSSIAN PIROZHKI

2 loaves Rhodes frozen white bread dough

1 lb. ground beef	4 c. cabbage, shredded
1 sm. onion	¼ c. water
1½ tsp. salt	½ tsp. caraway seed
1/8 tsp. pepper	

Follow 'regular instructions' on Rhodes package for thawing dough. Let rise once, then punch down and roll out into a big square on a lightly floured board. Cut into 16 or more 4-inch squares. Set aside. Cook ground beef until light brown; drain. Stir in cabbage, onion, water, salt, caraway seed, and pepper. Heat to boiling; reduce heat. Cover and simmer until cabbage is tender, 10 to 15 minutes. Place about ¼ cup filling on center of each square. Bring corners up and together; pinch to seal. Place seam side down on greased cookie sheets. Shape into rounds. Let rise until double, about 1 hour. Heat oven to 375°. Bake until light brown, 20 to 25 minutes. Brush tops with margarine. Can be cooked and frozen until a later date.

CHICKEN WITH CABBAGE AND APPLES

2 whole, skinless chicken breasts	½ tsp. black pepper
3 c. cabbage, sliced thick	2 T. margarine
2 unpeeled cooking apples, cored and cubed	
2 med. carrots, sliced	2 med. yellow onion, sliced
¼ c. unsweetened apple juice	1 T. brown sugar
1½ tsp. cider vinegar	¼ tsp. caraway seeds

Cut chicken breasts in half; sprinkle with pepper. Melt 1 T. margarine in 12-inch skillet. Add breasts and cook 2½ minutes on each side. Transfer to a platter. Add apples to skillet and cook on medium, until golden. Transfer to platter with chicken. Melt the remaining margarine in the skillet and add the cabbage, carrots, and onions; cook, stirring, until tender but still crisp – about 5 minutes. Stir in the apple juice, brown sugar, vinegar, and caraway seeds. Return the chicken and half the apples to the skillet. Reduce the heat to low, cover and simmer for 20 minutes. Transfer the chicken to a platter, ladle the sauce over it, and garnish with the reserved apples. Serves 4.

TRANSYLVANIAN GOULASH

3 lbs. sauerkraut, rinsed, drained and squeezed

6 slices bacon, diced	3 onions, chopped
3 cloves garlic, crushed	5 T. sweet Hungarian paprika
¼ tsp. cayenne pepper	2 T. caraway seeds

1 (29-oz.) can tomatoes, drained and chopped

2 c. chicken stock	1 c. sour cream

3 lbs. well-trimmed pork shoulder, cut into 1-inch cubes

2 T. flour	salt and pepper to taste

Squeeze sauerkraut as dry as possible. Set aside. Cook diced bacon until it is just about crisp and remove from pan. Add onions and garlic to bacon fat and cook until limp. Add the paprika, caraway seeds, cayenne pepper, salt, pepper, and reserved bacon; stir. Add tomatoes, pork and sauerkraut; stir. Pour enough chicken stock in to barely cover contents of pot. Simmer, covered, over low heat for about 1½ hours until pork is tender. With a wire whisk, stir flour into sour cream. Mix a bit of hot liquid from pot into sour cream, then pour sour cream mixture back into the goulash, stirring constantly. Simmer for additional 10 minutes, stirring occasionally. Serves 6.

BIEROCKS CASSEROLE

½ c. onion, chopped	1½ lb. lean ground beef
½ tsp. caraway seeds	

1 (16-oz.) can sauerkraut, drained and pressed dry

2 (8-oz.) cans refrigerated crescent rolls

1 (8-oz.) pkg. Cheddar cheese, shredded

Brown onion and ground beef in large skillet. Drain. Stir in drained sauerkraut and caraway seeds. Heat through and set aside. Press 1 pkg. of crescent roll dough into the bottom of a lightly greased 9 x 13 baking dish. Spread beef mixture on top, then lay 2nd pkg. of crescent roll dough over the top of the beef mixture. Press dough seams together and sprinkle with cheese. Bake in 350° oven for 25-30 minutes, or until golden brown. Serves 6.

CABBAGE WITH CRAB

1 lb. cabbage, shredded	1 T. oil
1 clove garlic, crushed	1 T. soy sauce
1 T. sherry	1 tsp. cornstarch
2 T. cabbage water	4 oz. canned crab meat

Cook shredded cabbage in salted, boiling water for 2 minutes. Drain, reserving 2 tablespoons of the water. Heat the oil and sauté the cabbage and garlic for 2 minutes. Add soy sauce, and sherry; mix well and cook for 1 minute. Mix the cornstarch to a smooth paste with the reserved cabbage water; stir into cabbage mixture. Add crab meat; stir well and cook for 1 minute to heat through.

SAUERKRAUT AND SAUSAGE BAKE

1½ lbs. bulk pork sausage
1 (29-oz.) can sauerkraut, rinsed, drained and snipped
1 T. green onion, sliced   4 T. grated Parmesan cheese
4 servings instant mashed potatoes

In skillet, brown sausage; drain off fat. Stir together sauerkraut and green onion; turn into a 1½ quart casserole. Spoon sausage over sauerkraut mixture. Prepare mashed potatoes according to package instructions. Stir 2 tablespoons of the cheese into potatoes. Spread potatoes over sausage; sprinkle with remaining 2 tablespoons cheese. Bake, uncovered, 400°, until heated through, 35 to 40 minutes. Serves 6.

REUBEN SANDWICHES

⅓ c. mayonnaise   1 T. bottled chili sauce
12 slices rye bread, buttered
½ lb. Swiss cheese, sliced
½ lb. cooked corned beef, sliced
1 (16-oz.) can sauerkraut, drained

Mix mayonnaise and chili sauce; spread on 6 slices of bread. Layer cheese, corned beef, and sauerkraut on slices; top with remaining slices of bread. Butter outside surfaces of sandwiches and grill. Serves 6.

FOILED FISH

1 (8-oz.) can sauerkraut, drained   1 c. tomatoes, diced
1 c. bread crumbs   1 c. onion, chopped
4 med. orange roughy, cod or tilapia fillets
4 T. butter   8 T. mayonnaise
4 12-inch squares of foil

Place fillets in center of each foil. On top of each fillet, place 2 tablespoons mayonnaise; top that with mixture of tomatoes, sauerkraut, and onion. Top off with bread crumbs and a pat of butter. Fold in the corners of the foil and place pouches on cookie sheet. Cook about 10 minutes on grill; rotate and continue to cook for about 10 more minutes.

MOM'S SAUERKRAUT AND RIBS

2 (20-oz.) cans sauerkraut, rinsed and drained
3 lbs. pork ribs   3 T. oil
¼ c. water   ½ tsp. caraway seeds
3 T. sugar   3 T. onions, chopped

Brown ribs under broiler for 15 minutes. Add sauerkraut, ribs, oil, water, caraway seeds, sugar, and onions to slow cooker. Cook on low for 8-10 hours.

PORK AND KRAUT

4 lbs. pork loin   1 T. caraway seeds
1 (29-oz.) can sauerkraut, rinsed and drained
¼ c. water   1 onion, sliced
1 lg. potato, sliced   1 lg. apple, peeled and sliced
1 (10 ¾-oz.) can cheddar cheese soup
salt and pepper to taste

In skillet, brown roast on all sides. Place in slow cooker. Combine sauerkraut, water, onion, potato, soup, caraway seeds, and apple. Pour over roast. Cover. Cook on low for 10 hours. Apple and potato will disappear into the soup to make a sauce. Serves 6.

REUBEN CASSEROLE

4 c. mashed potatoes   1 c. Swiss cheese, shredded

1 (16-oz.) can sauerkraut, rinsed and drained

4 green onions, sliced   paprika

2 c. cooked corned beef, diced

Place mashed potatoes in a bowl with sauerkraut and green onions; mix well. Spoon two-thirds into a greased 3-quart baking dish. Cover with the corned beef and cheese. Top with remaining mashed potatoes. Sprinkle with paprika. Bake, uncovered at 350° for 30 minutes, or until heated through. Serves 6-8.

KRAUT CHEESEBURGER

2 T. onion, chopped   2 T. green bell pepper, chopped

1 T. oil   1 c. sauerkraut, drained

1 c. bologna, or wieners, chopped

1 c. American cheese, grated   6 hamburger buns

Brown chopped onion and green pepper in oil. Add sauerkraut and bologna and cook for 5 more minutes. Stir in grated cheese. Cut hamburger buns in half and place ⅓ cup of the kraut mixture on each bun. Toast on a baking sheet under the broiler. Serves 6.

SAUERKRAUT MEAT LOAF

1 lb. ground beef   1 egg

1 c. sauerkraut, rinsed, drained and squeezed

¼ c. green bell pepper, finely chopped

½ c. regular oats, uncooked   ½ tsp. salt

½ tsp. pepper   ¼ c. catsup

Combine ground beef, sauerkraut, egg, bell pepper, oats, salt and pepper in a large bowl. Mix well. Put into an 8 x 8-inch microwavable baking dish. Spread catsup over the top. Cover with waxed paper and microwave on high for 10-15 minutes. Let rest 5 minutes before serving. Serves 6.

KRAUTED CHICKEN PARMESAN

2 lbs. chicken cutlets	2 eggs, beaten
1 c. bread crumbs	1 (15-oz.) can tomato sauce
1 (14-oz.) can sauerkraut, rinsed and drained	
¼ tsp. each of oregano, sage, thyme, and basil	
1½ c. mozzarella cheese	½ c. grated Parmesan cheese

Pound chicken until thin. Combine herbs and bread crumbs. Dip chicken into eggs and then into bread crumbs. Bake 400° 25 minutes, or until done. Pour tomato sauce over chicken and top with sauerkraut. Sprinkle with Parmesan cheese and bake at 350° for 20 minutes. Top with mozzarella cheese and bake until cheese is melted.

LEMON-CABBAGE ROLLS

6 cabbage leaves	1 lb. ground beef
¼ c. onion, chopped	1 clove garlic, minced
½ c. regular rice, uncooked	2 T. snipped parsley
1½ tsp. salt	¼ tsp. lemon pepper
¼ tsp. ground cinnamon	¼ tsp. dried oregano leaves
1½ c. water	½ c. shredded Swiss cheese
1 c. water	1 oz. chicken gravy mix
¾ c. water	2 tsp. lemon juice

Cover cabbage leaves with boiling water. Cook and stir ground beef, onions, and garlic until beef is light brown. Drain. Stir rice, parsley, 1½ tsp. salt, lemon pepper, cinnamon, oregano, 1½ cups water and cheese into beef. Heat to boiling; reduce heat. Cover and simmer, stirring occasionally, until water is absorbed, about 15 minutes. Heat oven to 350°. Dry cabbage leaves. Mound ½ cup filling at stem end of each cabbage leaf. Roll, folding in sides. Place in ungreased baking dish, 11-¾ x 7- ½ inches. Pour 1 cup water over cabbage rolls. Cover and bake 30 minutes. While this is cooking, mix chicken gravy mix, ¾ cup water, and 2 tsp. lemon juice. Heat to boiling, stirring occasionally. Pull cabbage rolls out when done; spoon lemon sauce over rolls and serve. Serves 6.

GERMAN CABBAGE ROLLS WITH GINGER SNAP SAUCE

1 lg. head cabbage	1 onion, chopped
1 lb. lean ground beef	½ c. uncooked rice
1 egg	¼ c. water
pinch garlic powder	salt and pepper to taste
1 c. sauerkraut, rinsed and drained	
½ c. raisins	3 T. sugar
2 T. brown sugar	1 T. lemon juice
1 (10-oz.) can beef broth	
3 ginger snaps, crushed into crumbs	

Wash cabbage and remove core. Cook cabbage in boiling water for 12 minutes. Carefully remove outer leaves (hopefully you will get 12 leaves). Set aside. Combine onion, beef, rice, egg, water, garlic powder, and seasonings; mix until well blended. Place about 2 tablespoons meat mixture on bottom of cabbage leaf. Tuck in sides and roll up. Place rolls in Dutch oven. Combine 1 cup drained sauerkraut, raisins, granulated sugar, brown sugar, lemon juice and beef broth; pour over cabbage rolls. Cover Dutch oven and cook about 1½ hours over low heat. Add crushed ginger snaps to sauce at the end of the cooking time to thicken the sauce. Makes approximately 12.

BEEF CABBAGE LOAF
(FINNISH LIHAKAALILAATIKKO)

8 c. head cabbage, shredded	¼ c. water
1 lb. ground beef	1 c. soft bread crumbs
½ c. milk	1 sm. onion, chopped
1 egg	1½ tsp. salt
¼ tsp. pepper	¼ tsp. dried marjoram leaves

Heat cabbage, water and ¼ teaspoon salt to boiling; reduce heat. Cover and simmer until cabbage is wilted, about 5 minutes; drain. Mix remaining ingredients. Place half the cabbage in ungreased 2-quart casserole. Spread beef mixture over cabbage; top with remaining cabbage. Cover and cook in 350° oven until done, 55-60 minutes. Serve with cranberry sauce. Serves 6.

HEARTY CASSEROLE

1 lb. ground beef	1 med. onion, chopped
1 (20-oz.) can tomatoes	¼ c. uncooked rice
1 sm. head cabbage, shredded	salt and pepper to taste

Brown meat and onion. Add cabbage, tomatoes, uncooked rice, and salt and pepper to taste. Mix well and put into a casserole dish. Cover and bake 1 hour at 350°.

GINGER PORK AND CABBAGE STIR-FRY

4 leaves bok choy	¼ c. sugar
¼ c. red wine vinegar	2 tsp. soy sauce
1 T. oil	1 c. carrots, sliced diagonally
1 lb. tenderloin, cut in half lengthwise, thin	
2 T. grated gingerroot	1 T. cornstarch
1 T. water	2 c. hot cooked rice

Slice leaves and stalks of bok choy into ½-inch pieces. Set aside. Combine sugar, vinegar, and soy sauce in small bowl; set aside. Heat oil in wok on medium-high. Add pork; cook and stir 5 minutes, until pork is no longer pink. Add bok choy and carrots; cook and stir until crisp-tender. Remove pork and vegetables from wok. Add gingerroot to wok; cook and stir 2 minutes. Add sugar-vinegar mixture; cook 2 minutes. Add pork and vegetables back to wok. In small bowl, blend cornstarch and water until smooth. Stir into pork and vegetable mixture and cook until mixture boils and thickens. Serve over hot rice.

CORNED BEEF AND CABBAGE

2 med. onions, sliced	3 lbs. corned beef brisket
1 c. apple juice	¼ c. brown sugar
2 tsp. orange peel, finely shredded	6 whole cloves
2 tsp. prepared mustard	6 cabbage wedges

Place onions in slow cooker. Place beef on top of onions. Combine apple juice, brown sugar, orange peel, cloves, and mustard. Pour over meat. Place cabbage on top. Cover. Cook on Low 10-12 hours, or High 5-6 hours. Serves 6.

SAVORY CABBAGE ROLLS

1 lg. head cabbage, cored and rinsed
1 lb. ground beef   ¾ c. onion, chopped
1 (15-oz.) can tomato sauce, divided
½ c. cooked white rice   ¾ tsp. salt
¼ tsp. pepper   1/8 tsp. dried oregano leaves
2 tsp. brown sugar   ¼ tsp. marjoram leaves
¼ tsp. dried oregano leaves

Place cabbage, cored-side down, in medium mixing bowl. Cover bowl with plastic wrap. Microwave on High for 4 to 5 minutes, or until outer leaves are pliable. Let stand for 5 minutes. Remove 8 large leaves. Refrigerate remaining cabbage in 1½ quart casserole, combine ground beef and onion. Microwave on High for 4 to 5 minutes, or until beef is no longer pink; stir once. Drain. Add ⅔ cup tomato sauce, rice, salt, pepper, and 1/8 teaspoon oregano. Mix well. Place about ½ cup beef mixture; roll up. Repeat with remaining cabbage leaves. Arrange rolls, seam-side-down, in 9-inch square baking dish. In small mixing bowl, blend remaining ingredients. Pour over cabbage rolls. Cover dish with plastic wrap. Microwave on High for 8 to 10 minutes, or until heated through and cabbage is tender; rotate dish once. Let stand for 5 minutes. Serves 4.

MINI REUBENS

1 (6 oz.) box rye melba toast rounds
¼ lb. cooked corned beef, thinly sliced
1 (8-oz.) can sauerkraut, rinsed, drained, and snipped
1 c. Swiss cheese, shredded
2 tsp. mustard   caraway seeds

Arrange 8 toast rounds on a dinner plate lined with paper towels. Cut corned beef into 1½-inch squares. Place on toast rounds. Top each with 1 teaspoon sauerkraut. Mix cheese with mustard. Place 1 teaspoon cheese mixture on top of sauerkraut on toast. Sprinkle with caraway seeds. Microwave 1 to 2 minutes on Medium, or until cheese melts. Repeat these steps with the rest of the toast rounds. Yields approximately 48 toast rounds.

HIDDEN REUBEN

3 c. Bisquick baking mix   ⅔ c. milk
2 T. margarine, softened   2 eggs
1 (12-oz.) can corned beef, finely chopped
1 (8-oz.) can sauerkraut, drained   ¼ c. mayonnaise
1 T. catsup   ½ c. Swiss cheese, shredded

Grease 12-cup Bundt cake pan. Mix Bisquick, milk, margarine, and eggs. Spread 2 cups of Bisquick mixture in bottom of greased cake Bundt pan. Sprinkle Swiss cheese over batter in pan. Mix corned beef, sauerkraut, mayonnaise, and catsup together. Spoon corned beef mixture onto center of batter in pan. Drop remaining batter by teaspoonfuls about ½-inch apart onto corned beef mixture. Bake 375° about 25 minutes, or until light brown and firm. Invert on heatproof serving plate. Serves 6.

SAUERKRAUT CORNED BEEF CRESCENTS

1 can refrigerated quick crescent rolls, separated into 8 triangles
1 c. sauerkraut, drained and squeezed
1 tsp. caraway seeds   8 slices cooked corned beef

Mix sauerkraut and caraway seeds together. Arrange triangles of dough on cookie sheet. Place a slice of meat on each triangle, top with 2 tablespoons of sauerkraut mixture and roll up to form crescents. Bake at 375° for about 10 minutes, or until light golden brown. Serves about 8.

GROUND BEEF WITH CABBAGE AND POTATOES

1 sm. head cabbage, cored and shredded
1 lb. ground beef   3 c. potatoes, sliced
1 T. butter   1 c. milk
salt and pepper to taste

Grease a baking dish. Arrange cabbage in baking dish. Top with potatoes, beef, and seasoning. Pour milk over top and bake at 350° for about 1 hour or until potatoes are tender and meat is thoroughly cooked. Serves 2-4.

MICROWAVE REUBEN SANDWICHES

4 slices dark rye bread   4 Swiss cheese sliced
4 cooked corned beef, thinly sliced
½ c. Thousand Island dressing
1 (8-oz.) can sauerkraut, rinsed, drained and squeezed

Place bread on a microwave safe tray, lined with paper towels. Top with corned beef. Spread dressing over corned beef; cover with sauerkraut and place cheese on top. Microwave, uncovered, on Low for 6-8 minutes, or until sandwich is heated through and cheese is melted. Serves 4.

REUBEN CORNED BEEF CASSEROLE

8 oz. cooked corned beef, shredded
2 eggs   ½ c. mayonnaise
¼ c. heavy whipping cream   1 tsp. dehydrated onion
½ tsp. dry mustard   2 tsp. caraway seeds
⅔ c. sauerkraut, rinsed and drained.
2 c. Swiss cheese, shredded

Grease 6-cup casserole and place corned beef in the bottom of it. Combine eggs, mayonnaise, whipping cream, onion, dry mustard, sauerkraut, and caraway seeds in a bowl. Pour this mixture over the corned beef and sprinkle cheese on top. Bake, covered, 30 minutes at 375° and then uncovered for 15 more minutes. Serves 4.

KIELBASA SAUSAGE WITH RED CABBAGE

1 lb. Kielbasa sausage, sliced   1/8 c. brown sugar
1 sm. head red cabbage, shredded ¼ tsp. salt
1 med. tart apple, peeled and shredded
1/8 c. cider vinegar   1/8 c. onion, chopped
½ tsp. grated lemon peel   ¼ tsp. caraway seeds

Combine all ingredients, except sausage, in a 2-quart glass casserole. Cover. Microwave on High for 7-10 minutes, stirring twice. Piece sausage thoroughly and arrange on top of cabbage. Cover. Microwave on High 10-14 minute, or until heated through. Serves 4.

STUFFED CABBAGE

4 c. water	12 lg. cabbage leaves
1 lb. lamb or turkey	½ c. cooked rice
½ tsp. salt	1/8 tsp. pepper
¼ tsp. dried thyme	¼ tsp. nutmeg
¼ tsp. cinnamon	¾ c. water
1 (6-oz.) can tomato paste	

Boil 4 cups water in saucepan. Remove saucepan from heat. Soak cabbage leaves in hot water for 5 minutes, or until softened. Drain water from leaves. Cool. Combine ground turkey or lamb, rice, salt, pepper, thyme, nutmeg, and cinnamon. Place 2 tablespoons of mixture on each leaf. Roll up firmly. Stack rolls in slow cooker. Combine tomato paste and ¾ cup water until smooth. Pour over rolls. Cover. Cook on Low 6-8 hours. Serves 6.

CHICKEN REUBEN BAKE

4 boneless, skinless chicken-breast halves
2 lb. pkg. sauerkraut, rinsed and drained
5 slices Swiss cheese
1¼ c. Thousand Island salad dressing
2 T. fresh parsley, chopped

Place chicken in slow cooker. Layer sauerkraut over chicken and then layer cheese. Top with salad dressing. Sprinkle with parsley. Cover. Cook on Low 6-8 hours. Serves 4.

SWEET AND SOUR CABBAGE

3 slices bacon	4 c. cabbage, shredded
2 T. cider vinegar	2 tsp. Splenda
1/8 tsp. red pepper flakes	

In skillet, cook bacon until crisp. Remove bacon to a dish. Add cabbage to skillet and sauté cabbage in bacon grease until tender-crisp. Stir in vinegar, red pepper flakes, Splenda, and crumbled bacon. Serve. Serves 4.

QUICK CORNED BEEF AND CABBAGE

2 med. potatoes, thinly sliced (about 2 cups)
1 med. onion, sliced   ¼ c. water
¾ tsp. salt   1/8 tsp. pepper
1 (12-oz.) can corned beef, crumbled
½ head cabbage, cut into wedges (about 1¼ lb.)
¼ c. butter, melted

Grease 3-quart glass casserole dish. Layer potatoes and onions in dish; add water, salt and pepper. Heat, covered, on High in microwave 8 to 9 minutes. Add corned beef and cabbage; pour butter over cabbage. Heat, covered, on High 10 to 12 minutes, or until cabbage is tender; turning dish once. Let stand 5 minutes before serving. Serves 4.

EASY HAM AND CABBAGE

1½ c. ham, finely chopped   4 c. cabbage, shredded
⅓ c. Minute rice, uncooked   ½ c. onion, chopped
1 (15-oz.) can Hunt's Chunky Tomato Sauce
2 tsp. prepared mustard   2 T. brown sugar
¼ tsp. black pepper

Combine ham, cabbage, uncooked rice, and onion in a 8-cup glass bowl. Add tomato sauce, mustard, brown sugar, and black pepper; mix well. Cover and microwave on High for 12-15 minutes, or until cabbage and rice are tender, stirring after 6 minutes. Serves 4.

PORK ROAST WITH SAUERKRAUT

2 3-lb. pork shoulder roasts
1 (29-oz.) can sauerkraut, rinsed and drained
½ tsp. caraway seeds   ¼ c. brown sugar
1 env. dry onion soup mix   ½ c. water

Place roasts in slow-cooker. Combine sauerkraut, brown sugar, and onion soup mix; layer over roasts. Pour water over all. Cover. Cook on Low 7 hours. Serves 8.

JACK RIVER FLAPJACKS

2 eggs	2½ c. milk
1½ c. whole-wheat flour	1 c. white flour
2 T. sugar	2 tsp. baking powder
1 tsp. baking soda	1 tsp. salt
¼ c. oil	

½ c. sauerkraut, rinsed, drained, snipped and squeezed

Grease and heat griddle Mix all ingredients in bowl. Pour batter by ¼ cupfuls onto hot griddle. Cook until golden brown. Yields about 20 pancakes.

SAUERKRAUT SURPRISES

1 c. sauerkraut, drained, snipped and squeezed

1 c. cooked corned beef, chopped

1 c. bread crumbs	1 egg
¼ c. onion, chopped	2 T. parsley
1 tsp. prepared horseradish	1 clove garlic, crushed
½ tsp. salt	¼ c. water

Mix sauerkraut, corned beef, onion, parsley, horseradish, garlic, and salt together. Dip sauerkraut balls into egg mixture, and then roll in bread crumbs. Bake on ungreased bake sheet about 20 minutes at 400°. Serve hot with mustard.

MOM'S SAUERKRAUT OMELET

1½ T. butter, divided	1 tsp. onion, chopped

1 tsp. green pepper, chopped

¼ c. sauerkraut, rinsed, drained and squeezed

2 eggs, well beaten

Melt 1 tablespoon butter in 6-inch skillet. Sauté green peppers, onions, and sauerkraut until onions are tender. Remove from skillet. Melt remainder of butter in skillet; add eggs and cook until set. Lay the vegetable mixture on ½ of the omelet and fold the other ½ over it. Let cook for 1 minute, or until vegetables are heated through. Serves 1.

MUSHROOM AND BARLEY STUFFED CABBAGE ROLLS

1 lg. head cabbage	2 (14-oz.) cans tomato sauce
4 T. olive oil	1 lg. onion, chopped
4 cloves garlic, minced	1½ tsp. paprika
1/8 c. red wine	salt and pepper to taste
1 c. cooked quick barley	4 T. butter
½ lb. fresh mushrooms, washed and chopped	

Place whole head of cabbage in large pot. Pour boiling water over it. In a few minutes the leaves will soften. Gently peel off 14 leaves. If leaves are not pliable, soak in boiling water again. Set aside. Heat olive oil in large skillet and sauté onions, garlic, and paprika until garlic is golden. Add tomato sauce, red wine, salt and pepper; simmer sauce until thickened, at least 30 minutes. Set aside. Sauté chopped mushrooms in 4 tablespoons of butter; add salt and pepper, and mix in cooked barley to heat. Place 2 rounded tablespoons of mushroom-barley mixture on softened cabbage leaf and roll up. Repeat until you are out of leaves. Lightly butter shallow baking dish. Put a few spoonfuls of sauce in the bottom. Arrange cabbage rolls in one layer in the dish. Pour remaining sauce over rolls. Bake at 350° for about 40 minutes. Serves 7.

WIENERWURST

1 1-lb. pkg. sauerkraut, rinsed, drained and squeezed dry

1 T. shortening	½ c. beer

salt, pepper, brown sugar to taste

1 pkg. hot dogs	1 sm. onion, sliced
1 tsp. caraway seeds	1 pkg. hot dog buns
1 cooking apple, cored and diced	

Heat shortening in saucepan; add onion and cook until tender. Stir in sauerkraut, caraway seeds and beer. Cover and simmer 15 minutes. Add apple, brown sugar, salt, pepper, and hot dogs; simmer until hot dogs are heated through. Spoon hot dog mixture on buns.

GERMAN SIMMERED SAUERKRAUT AND PORK

½ c. dried apple slices   1 c. onions, diced

3 bacon slices, diced   1 tsp. oil

2 c. sauerkraut, rinsed and drained

1 c. chicken broth   1/8 tsp. fennel seeds

1/8 tsp. caraway seeds   4 pork chops

Place apples in small bowl; cover with hot water and let stand 5 minutes. Drain. In a Dutch oven, over medium heat, sauté onions and bacon in the oil for 5 minutes. Add sauerkraut, broth, fennel seeds, caraway seeds, and apples. Cover and simmer 10 minutes. Cook pork chops in a frying pan until browned on both sides. Transfer chops to Dutch oven; cover and simmer until chops are cooked through, 10-20 minutes. Serves 4.

OLD WORLD SAUERKRAUT SUPPER

3 slices bacon, cut into small pieces

2 T. flour   2 (15-oz.) cans sauerkraut

2 sm. potatoes, cubed   2 sm. apples, cubed

3 T. brown sugar   1½ tsp. caraway seeds

3 lbs. Polish sausage, cut into 3-inch pieces

½ c. water

Fry bacon until crisp. Drain, reserving drippings. Add flour to bacon drippings. Blend well. Stir in sauerkraut and bacon. Transfer to a slow cooker. Add potatoes, apples, brown sugar, caraway seeds, Polish sausage, and water. Cover. Cook on Low 6-8 hours, or High 3-4 hours. Serves 8.

MATANUSKA VALLEY CREAM CAN DINNER

15 sm. potatoes	15 sm. carrots
2 heads cabbage, cut into wedges	
15 ½ ears of corn	5 cloves garlic, minced
1 c. onions, chopped	1 can beer

every kind of link sausage you can find. (Kielbasa, Polish, etc.)

Clean out 8 gallon cream can. Set an opened can of beer in the bottom of the cream can. Wrap corn in tin foil with a pat of butter in each pouch. Put into cream can, around opened beer can. Next, put in 15 small potatoes on top of the corn. Add 15 small carrots on top of the potatoes. Tie chopped onions and minced garlic in cheesecloth and add to cream can. Add enough sausage to feed 15 people. Add 1 potato to top for testing purposes. Put on lid, but leave a small hole, or opening for steam. Steam over an outside propane stove for 1½ hours. When top potato is cooked, dinner is ready.

Desserts

DESSERTS

SAUERKRAUT FUDGE

2 c. sugar	1 c. brown sugar
1 c. sauerkraut, rinsed, drained, snipped and squeezed	
1 c. canned pineapple juice	½ c. milk
1 T. corn syrup	¼ tsp. salt
2 T. margarine	24 lg. marshmallows
1 tsp. coconut extract	1 c. walnuts, chopped

Combine sugars, canned pineapple juice, sauerkraut, milk, corn syrup, salt, and butter in a 2-quart saucepan. Stir occasionally. Cook to soft-ball stage (238°, if it starts to burn. When it hits soft-ball stage, remove and add marshmallows, and vanilla. Mix to melt marshmallows, then beat until mixture becomes creamy and heavy. Add nuts. Spread in a buttered 8-inch square pan. Cut into small squares when cool and firm. Makes 48 pieces.

MOLASSES CACHE COOKIES

½ c. margarine or shortening	½ c. sugar
1 egg	1 c. molasses
½ c. sauerkraut, rinsed, drained, snipped and squeezed	
3 ½ c. flour	1 tsp. cinnamon
¾ tsp. ground cloves	½ tsp. ginger
2 tsp. baking soda	½ tsp. salt
¼ c. boiling water	

Cream margarine and sugar. Add egg, molasses, and sauerkraut. Add flour, cinnamon, cloves, ginger, and baking soda to creamed mixture. Add boiling water and mix. Drop by rounded teaspoonfuls onto greased cookie sheets. Dip spoon or cookie scoop in warm water if batter is too sticky. Bake 350° 12 to 15 minutes, or until set.

FAUX BANANA CAKE

3 eggs	½ c. shortening
1 ⅔ c. sugar	⅔ c. milk
2 tsp. lemon juice	2 ¼ c. flour
1¼ tsp. baking soda	1¼ tsp. baking powder
1 tsp. salt	2 tsp. banana extract

1¼ c. sauerkraut, rinsed, drained, snipped and squeezed
⅔ c. walnuts, chopped

In large bowl, mix eggs, shortening, and sugar. Add milk and lemon juice; mix. Add flour, baking soda, baking powder, salt and banana extract. Mix well. Stir in sauerkraut and walnuts. Put mixture into 9 x 13-inch baking pan and bake 350° 35 to 45 minutes. Frost with Vanilla Butter Frosting. Serves 12.

Vanilla Butter Frosting

⅓ c. margarine, softened	3 c. powdered sugar
1½ tsp. vanilla extract	2 T. milk

Beat all ingredients together, and frost cake.

DENALI DESSERT

½ c. margarine	1 c. nuts, chopped
1½ c. graham cracker crumbs	1 c. peanut butter chips

1 (14-oz.) can sweetened condensed milk
1 c. semi-sweet chocolate chips
1 c. sauerkraut, rinsed, drained, snipped and squeezed
whipped topping

Preheat oven to 350°. In a 9 x 13 baking pan, melt margarine in oven. Sprinkle crumbs over margarine; pour sweetened condensed milk over crumbs. Sprinkle chopped sauerkraut over crumbs and milk. Sprinkle chocolate chips and then peanut butter chips over mixture. Top with nuts. Press ingredients down in pan with hand or big spoon. Bake 25 to 30 minutes or until lightly browned. Keep refrigerated. Serve with a dollop of whipped topping on top of each serving. Serves 12.

BEAVER HUTS

12 squares almond bark   ¼ c. margarine
16 lg. marshmallows   2½ c. quick cooking oats
½ c. sauerkraut, rinsed, drained, chopped and squeezed
½ tsp. anise extract

In saucepan, over low heat, melt 12 squares Almond Bark, margarine, and marshmallows; stir until smooth. Stir in oats sauerkraut, and ½ teaspoon of anise extract. Drop by teaspoonfuls onto wax paper-lined baking sheets. Store in freezer to keep firm.

MUSHER'S FUDGE

1 1-lb. box powdered sugar   ½ c. cocoa
¼ tsp. salt   1 T. milk
1 c. sauerkraut, rinsed, drained, chopped and squeezed
2 tsp. vanilla extract   1 tsp. mint extract
½ c. margarine   1 c. walnuts, chopped

In 1½-quart casserole stir sugar, cocoa, salt, milk, sauerkraut, vanilla extract, and mint extract together. Mixture will be very dry. Put ½ cup margarine on top of these mixed ingredients. Microwave on High 2 minutes. Stir vigorously until all is mixed. Blend in nuts. Pour into a lightly buttered, bread pan. Chill 1 hour in the refrigerator before serving. If too much fluid was left in sauerkraut, fudge will soft set. Put in freezer to firm up. Makes about 36 squares.

ICE BOX CANYON PIE

1 graham cracker pie crust   3 c. mini marshmallows
½ c. canned coconut milk   1½ c. frozen whip topping
1 c. sauerkraut, rinsed, drained, snipped and squeezed as dry as possible
½ c. pineapple, apricot, or peach jam
2 graham crackers, crushed

In saucepan, combine milk and marshmallows. Cook and stir until marshmallows are melted. Remove from heat, fold in whipped topping, sauerkraut, and jam. Pour into crust. Sprinkle crushed graham crackers over top and freeze. To serve, thaw 5 minutes. Serves 8.

HOOTCH CAKE

½ lb. margarine	1 c. sugar
2 eggs	2 tsp. vanilla extract
½ c. sauerkraut, rinsed, drained, snipped, and squeezed	
½ c. milk	1/8 tsp. nutmeg
2 c. flour	2 tsp. baking powder
whipped topping	

Cream margarine and sugar with mixer. Add eggs, vanilla, sauerkraut and milk. Mix in nutmeg, flour, and baking powder. Pour batter into greased 11 x 13-inch baking pan. Bake 350° 30 to 40 minutes, or until toothpick comes out clean. Pour syrup over cake. Serves 15.

Syrup for Hootch Cake

1 c. water	1 c. sugar
4 cloves	1 stick cinnamon
¾ c. white rum	

Make syrup by mixing water, sugar, and spices. Bring to a boil and boil 5 minutes. Remove from heat; add rum. Remove cloves and cinnamon stick from syrup. Pour only 1 cup of syrup over cake. Cake is better the next day. Top each piece of cake with a dollop of whipped topping.

HOMESTEAD GINGERBREAD

1½ c. flour	¼ tsp. baking soda
1½ tsp. ginger	1½ tsp. cinnamon
½ tsp. cloves	¼ tsp. salt
2 eggs	½ c. molasses
½ c. milk	½ c. margarine, melted
½ c. sauerkraut, rinsed, drained, snipped and squeezed	
½ c. sugar	

Grease 8-inch square pan. Combine all ingredients in large bowl and mix well. Bake 350° 25 to 30 minutes.

Hard Sauce for Homestead Gingerbread

1 lb. powdered sugar	½ c. margarine, melted
¼ tsp. salt	¼ c. rum

Combine sugar, salt and rum in 1½ quart casserole dish. Place butter on top. Microwave on High 1½ to 2 minutes. Beat on High with Mixer until smooth. Can use ¼ cup milk with 2 tsp. rum flavoring in place of rum.

SAUERKRAUT-OATMEAL BARS

½ c. walnuts, chopped	1½ c. rolled oats
1 c. brown sugar	¼ tsp. salt
1½ c. flour	1 c. shortening or margarine
¼ tsp. baking soda	1½ c. sugar
1½ c. sauerkraut, rinsed, drained, snipped and squeezed	
2 T. cornstarch	¼ c. water
1 tsp. vanilla extract	1 tsp. rum extract
Cool Whip	

Combine nuts, oats, brown sugar, salt, flour, shortening, and baking soda. Mix until crumbly. Pat ½ of mixture into 9 x 13 baking pan. In saucepan, combine sauerkraut, granulated sugar, cornstarch and water. Cook for 10 minutes on medium, or until sugar is dissolved. Remove from heat; add vanilla and rum extracts. Pour this sauce over crust in pan. Sprinkle with remainder of crumb mixture. Bake 350° for 20-30 minutes. Serve with a big dollop of Cool Whip on each serving. Serves 12.

IMPOSSIBLE SAUERKRAUT PIE

4 eggs	½ c. flour
2 c. milk	1 c. sugar
1 tsp. vanilla extract	1 tsp. coconut extract
½ c. margarine	
1 c. sauerkraut, rinsed, drained, snipped and squeezed	

Mix all in a blender. Pour into a greased 10-inch pie plate. Bake 350° 45 minutes to 60 minutes, until set. Serves 8.

BOOTLEGGER RAISIN-KRAUT BARS

3 c. raisins	⅓ c. rum
¼ c. water	⅓ c. margarine, softened
⅓ c. brown sugar	1 c. flour

½ sauerkraut, rinsed, drained, snipped and squeezed
1 c. walnuts, chopped
1 (14-oz.) can sweetened condensed milk

Mix margarine and brown sugar in medium bowl. Stir in flour until well blended. Press mixture into bottom of a greased 9 x 13 baking pan. Bake 10 minutes. In small saucepan, combine raisins, rum, and water. Simmer for 5 minutes to soften raisins. Remove from heat. Add sauerkraut and nuts to saucepan and mix well. Spread this mixture over crust in pan. Pour sweetened condensed milk over mixture. Bake 350° 30 minutes, or until topping is golden brown. Cool in pan 15 minutes. Cut into squares. Store in refrigerator to keep firm. Makes 4 dozen

MINER'S BARS

2 eggs	¼ c. shortening
1 tsp. vanilla	¾ c. brown sugar
¾ c. flour	¼ tsp. salt

½ c. sauerkraut, rinsed, drained, snipped and squeezed
½ c. walnuts, chopped

Mix together eggs, shortening, vanilla and brown sugar. Add flour, salt, sauerkraut and walnuts. Pour batter into an 8-inch square baking pan. Bake 375° 25 minutes. Yields 16 squares.

Maple Frosting for Miner's Bars

2 c. powdered sugar	¼ c. margarine, softened
1 T. milk	1 tsp. maple flavoring

Mix all ingredients together. Put on cake, when cake is cool.

.

AUTUMN PUMPKIN CAKE

3 large eggs	¾ c. brown sugar
½ c. flour	½ tsp. ground cinnamon
¼ tsp. ground allspice	¼ tsp. ground cardamom
¼ tsp. ginger	¼ tsp. nutmeg
¼ tsp. salt	1 tsp. baking powder
½ c. canned pumpkin purée	½ c. walnuts, chopped

1 c. sauerkraut, rinsed, drained, snipped and squeezed

½ tsp. vanilla extract	whipped topping

Grease 8-inch square baking pan. In large bowl, mix eggs and brown sugar. Add flour, spices, salt, baking powder, pumpkin, sauerkraut to bowl and mix well. Add nuts and vanilla; mix. Bake 375° 30 to 35 minutes, or until top is well browned. Serve warm with whipped topping. Serves 6.

GOLD DUST CAKE

2 eggs	¾ c. sugar
¼ tsp. salt	1 c. flour
1 tsp. baking powder	1 tsp. dried lemon peel

1 c. sauerkraut, rinsed, drained, snipped and squeezed

½ c. hot milk	2 T. butter
1 tsp. lemon extract	5 drops yellow food coloring

Grease 8-inch square pan. In large bowl, beat eggs and sugar. Add all other ingredients and mix well. Bake 350° 30 minutes. Serves 6.

Lemon Frosting for Gold Dust Cake

2½ c. powdered sugar	¼ c. milk
3 T. margarine, softened	1½ tsp. lemon extract

Mix all ingredients and frost cooled cake.

WINTER PINEAPPLE PUDDING

1 ¾ c. water   1 c. sugar
½ c. sauerkraut, rinsed, drained, snipped and squeezed
½ c. crushed pineapple, drained ¼ c. cornstarch
1 tsp. coconut extract   whipped topping
cardamom

Heat 1 ¾ cups water and 1 cup sugar to boiling, stirring occasionally. Add sauerkraut, and pineapple and cook 2 minutes to heat through. Mix ¼ cup water and cornstarch; stir into sauerkraut mixture. Heat to boiling, stirring constantly. Boil and stir 1 minute. Stir in coconut extract. Refrigerate until ready to serve. Serve with dollops of whipped topping sprinkled with cardamom. Serves 6.

POT HOLE CRUNCH

1 c. sauerkraut, rinsed, drained, snipped and squeezed
¾ c. sugar   2 T. flour
1 tsp. cinnamon   1 tsp. grated orange rind
2 tsp. vanilla   1 c. flour
2 T. sugar   2 tsp. baking powder
½ tsp. salt   ¼ c. butter
1 egg, well beaten   3 T. milk
2 T. orange juice   1 T. sugar
whipped topping or ice cream

Grease 9-inch square pan. Spread sauerkraut in pan. Sprinkle with mixture of ¾ cup sugar, 2 tablespoons flour, cinnamon, grated orange rind, and vanilla. In a bowl, mix 1 cup flour, 2 tablespoons sugar, baking powder, salt, and butter. It will resemble cornmeal. Add egg and milk to the bowl; mix. Spread bowl mixture on top of sauerkraut mixture with spatula. Bake 350° 35 minutes. While it is baking, mix 2 tablespoons of orange juice and 1 tablespoon of sugar. When cake comes out of oven, pour the orange juice mixture on cake. Serve crunch with whipped topping or ice cream on top. Serves 6.

CHOCOLATE SAUERKRAUT CAKE

2 ¼ c. flour	1 tsp. baking powder
½ tsp. salt	1 tsp. baking soda
½ c. cocoa	⅔ c. shortening
1½ c. brown sugar	1½ tsp. vanilla extract
1 c. water	3 eggs
1 tsp. cinnamon	¼ tsp. almond extract
1 c. sauerkraut, rinsed, drained, snipped and squeezed	

Mix all together, put into a greased 9 x 13 baking pan and bake at 375° for 35 minutes. Serves 12.

Frosting for Chocolate Sauerkraut Cake

5 T. flour	1 c. milk
1 c. sugar	1 c. margarine
2 tsp. almond extract	

Blend flour and milk. Cook to thick paste, stirring constantly. Let cool. Cream margarine, sugar, and almond extract in bowl until fluffy. Gradually add four/milk paste. Beat 10 minutes until consistency of whipped cream.

SIMPLE RASPBERRY-KRAUT PIE

2 pie crusts, uncooked	¼ c. water
¼ c. cornstarch	
1 c. sauerkraut, rinsed, drained, chopped and squeezed	
1 (16-oz.) jar raspberry jam	½ tsp. almond extract
2 tsp. butter	vanilla ice cream

In cup, mix ¼ cup water with ¼ cup cornstarch. In bowl, mix sauerkraut, raspberry jam, and almond extract. Add cornstarch mixture and mix all. Dump into pie crust. Dot with 1 teaspoons butter. Put top crust on. Cut slits for venting steam. Bake 375° 45 minutes, or until golden brown. Serve with vanilla ice cream to compliment tartness. Serves 8.

SURPRISE CAKE

4 egg whites	1½ c. sugar
½ c. shortening	1 c. milk
2 c. flour	3 ½ tsp. baking powder
1 tsp. salt	1 tsp. vanilla extract
2 tsp. coconut extract	

1 c. sauerkraut, rinsed, drained, snipped and squeezed

Mix egg whites, sugar, and shortening in large bowl. Add milk; mix. Add flour, baking powder, salt, vanilla and coconut extracts; mix well. Fold in sauerkraut. Pour into greased 9 x 13 baking pan. Bake 350° 45 to 50 minutes, or until toothpick comes out clean. Frost with Chocolate Frosting. Serves 12.

Chocolate Frosting for Surprise Cake

½ c. margarine, softened	⅔ c. cocoa
3 c. powdered sugar	⅓ c. milk
1 tsp. vanilla extract	

CABIN FEVER CHERRY CAKE

2 c. flour	¼ c. granulated sugar
½ c. shortening	3 tsp. baking powder
1 egg, slightly beaten	⅔ c. milk
2 c. sauerkraut	1 (6-oz.) pkg. cherry Jell-O
½ c. flour	¼ c. margarine
1½ c. granulated sugar	vanilla ice cream

Combine flour, sugar, and baking powder; add shortening. Mix as for pie crust. Add beaten egg and milk. Mix well. Spread dough into a 9 x 13-inch greased pan. Sprinkle sauerkraut on top of dough. Sprinkle package of Jell-O over sauerkraut. Mix ½ cup floor, ¼ cup margarine, and 1½ cups sugar together in small bowl; sprinkle this over the Jell-O. Bake 350° 35-45 minutes. Cut in squares when cool. Serve with a scoop of vanilla ice cream on top.

TUNDRA SQUARES

2 egg whites	4 T. oil
½ c. orange juice concentrate, thawed	
1 c. sugar	½ c. flour
1 tsp. baking soda	1 tsp. baking powder
½ tsp. salt	1 tsp. cinnamon
1 c. sauerkraut, rinsed, drained, snipped and squeezed	
½ c. walnuts, chopped	

Mix sugar, oil, orange juice concentrate, and egg whites in a large bowl. Add flour, baking soda, baking powder, salt, and cinnamon; mix well. Fold in sauerkraut and walnuts. Pour into a 9 x 13 baking pan. Bake 350° 40 to 45 minutes, or until toothpick comes out clean. Frost with Orange Frosting. Serves 12.

Orange Frosting for Tundra Squares

1 lb. powdered sugar	¼ tsp. salt
1 tsp. orange extract	1/8 c. milk
⅓ c. margarine, softened	

Mix all ingredients in small bowl. Frost cake.

SPICY SAUERKRAUT CAKE

3 eggs	½ c. oil
1½ c. sugar	⅓ c. water
2 c. flour	1¼ tsp. baking soda
1 tsp. salt	1½ tsp. cinnamon
1¼ tsp. ground cloves	1¼ tsp. ground nutmeg
1 tsp. vanilla extract	
2 c. sauerkraut, rinsed, drained, snipped and squeezed	

Good

Beat eggs, oil, sugar, and water in large bowl. Add flour, baking soda, salt, cinnamon, ground cloves, ground nutmeg and vanilla. Mix well. Fold in sauerkraut. Pour batter into a greased 9 x 13 baking pan. Bake 350° 45 to 50 minutes. Frost with Penuche Frosting. Serves 12

Penuche Frosting for Spicy Sauerkraut Cake

½ c. margarine	1 c. brown sugar
¼ c. milk	2 c. powdered sugar

Melt margarine and brown sugar in medium saucepan. Boil 2 minutes. Stir in milk, boil, and remove from heat. Cool. Add powdered sugar; beat until spreading consistency.

TRAIL COOKIES

1 c. sauerkraut, rinsed, drained, snipped and squeezed

¾ c. margarine, softened	1 c. brown sugar
½ c. granulated sugar	1 egg
1 tsp. vanilla	¼ c. milk
1 c. flour	1 tsp. cinnamon
½ tsp. baking soda	¼ tsp. salt
3 c. rolled oats	½ c. raisins (optional)

Mix together margarine, sugars, egg, vanilla and milk. Add flour, cinnamon, baking soda, and salt. Add oatmeal and sauerkraut. Drop by 1/8 cupfuls onto greased baking sheet. Bake 350° 12 to 15 minutes. Yields 28 cookies.

BERRY GOOD PIE

2 pie crusts, uncooked	1 T. butter

2 c. fresh blueberries, or 2 cups drained frozen berries

1½ c. sauerkraut, rinsed, drained, chopped and squeezed

¼ c. 1-Minute Tapioca, uncooked	vanilla ice cream
1½ c. sugar	½ tsp. cinnamon

Mix blueberries and sauerkraut in a bowl. Add tapioca, sugar, cinnamon and mix with spoon. Dump into pie crust in pie pan. Dot with butter. Put top crust on pie. Cut 6 small slits in top crust to vent. Brush top crust with milk. Sprinkle with a little sugar. Bake 375° 45 minutes, or until golden brown. Serve with vanilla ice cream to compliment tartness of pie.

PINA COLADA CAKE

½ c. shortening ¼ c. oil
3 eggs 1¼ c. sugar
1 c. water 2 c. flour
3 ½ tsp. baking powder ½ tsp. salt
½ c. crushed pineapple, undrained
½ c. sauerkraut, rinsed, drained and squeezed
1 T. coconut extract

Mix shortening, oil, eggs, sugar, and water together. Add flour, baking powder, salt. Add crushed pineapple, sauerkraut and coconut extract. Mix well. Pour into a greased Bundt pan and bake 350° 40 to 45 minutes. Drizzle with glaze. Serves 12.

Glaze for Pina Colada Cake

1 c. powdered sugar ½ tsp. coconut extract
1 T. hot water

NO COCONUT-NO PROBLEM PIE

1 c. sugar 6 T. flour
¼ tsp. salt 2 c. milk
2 egg yolks, beaten 1 tsp. coconut extract
2 T. butter
1 c. sauerkraut, rinsed, drained, chopped and squeezed
1 graham cracker crust whipped topping

In saucepan, mix sugar, flour and salt. Add a little of the milk to make a paste. Add the rest of the milk. Cook on medium, stirring often, until thick. Add a little of the hot mixture to beaten egg yolks. Pour back into the saucepan and cook a few more minutes. Add the butter, sauerkraut, and extract. Dump mixture into blender and blend on Chop for 45 seconds. Pour into graham cracker crust and refrigerate until set. Top with whipped topping. Serves 8.

SLUICE-BOX PIE

2 pie crusts, uncooked   1½ c. water
1¼ c. sugar   1½ tsp. cream of tartar
1 tsp. cinnamon   1/8 tsp. ground ginger
¼ c. water   3 T. cornstarch
1½ c. sauerkraut, rinsed, drained, chopped and squeezed
2 tsp. butter

Combine 1½ cups water, sugar, cream of tartar, cinnamon, ground ginger in small saucepan. In cup, mix ¼ cup water and 3 tablespoons cornstarch. Add cornstarch mixture to ingredients in saucepan. Cook and stir on Medium-High until thickened. Spread sauerkraut over bottom of 1 pie crust in pie pan. Pour thickened sauce over sauerkraut in pie pan. Dot with 2 teaspoons butter. Put top pie crust on. Brush milk over surface of pie crust and sprinkle with a little sugar. Cut slits in top crust to vent pie. Bake 375° 45 minutes, or until golden brown. Serve with a scoop of vanilla ice cream. Serves 8.